The Path of Knowledge
or
The Path of Ignorance?

A small brief treatise discussing a blessing from the blessings of Allāh:
(Knowledge & Islam).

Project Madrasah Dār SEMA

`alamiyyah Academic Structured Islamic Education
If Allah wants good for you He will grant you understanding of the Religion.
Knowledge. Action. Invitation to the Message. Patience.

Knowledge
Modular Education For Higher Madrassah Academic Development & Thinking
The Academic `alamiyyah Seminary Programme & Title Certification

`aqidah * fiqh * hadith * tafsir * Arabic * `usul * da`wah * other Sciences

Private Education

*Another book for study. This is a very basic level for your academic madrasah education part of the early Higher Madrasah Education programme. We ask **Allāh** that He allows you to benefit from this small brief treatise & that He allows it to be a cause of guidance for the entire globe.*

1 Private Education - **Project Madrasah Dār SEMA** - *Make your notes using the blank space below:*

The Path of Knowledge or The Path of Ignorance?

*A small brief treatise discussing a blessing from the blessings of **Allāh**: (Knowledge).*

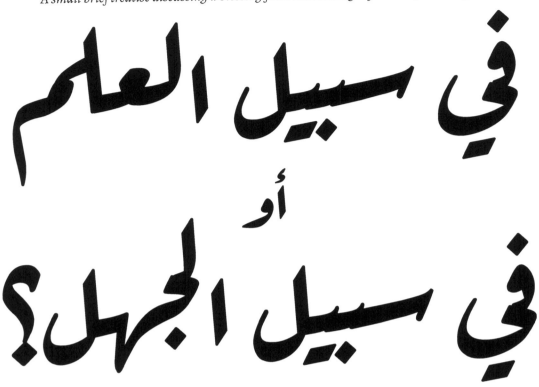

في سبيل العلم

أو

في سبيل الجهل؟

(باللغة الإنجليزية)

البرنامج العالمي الأكاديمي - دراسة خاصة

تأليف الفقير إلى الله:

خادم الدين بن يونس بن عبد القادر

السريع

غفر الله له ولوالديه وللمسلمين

مشروع دار عقيدة الإسلام للنشر والتوزيع

The Path of Knowledge or The Path of Ignorance?

*A small brief treatise discussing a blessing from the blessings of **Allāh**: (Knowledge).*

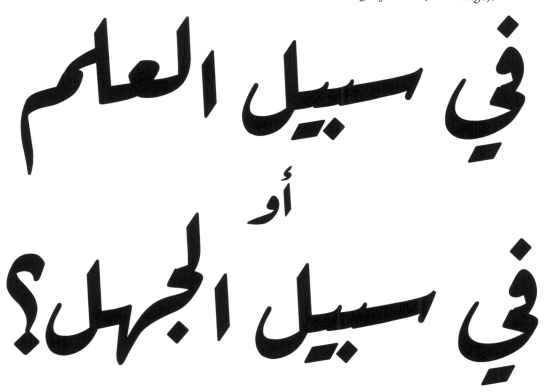

في سبيل العلم

أو

في سبيل الجهل؟

(باللغة الإنجليزية)

البرنامج العالمي الأكاديمي - دراسة خاصة

تأليف الفقير إلى الله:

خادم الدين بن يونس بن عبد القادر السريع

غفر الله له ولوالديه وللمسلمين

مشروع دار عقيدة الإسلام للنشر والتوزيع

The Path of Knowledge or The Path of Ignorance?

*A small brief treatise discussing a blessing from the blessings of **Allāh**: (Knowledge).*

بِسْمِ اللّٰهِ الرَّحْمٰنِ الرَّحِيمِ

إنما الأعمال بالنيات

Indeed All Actions Are Judged by Intentions

Private Education
We also offer online lessons.

Join or Support.

How do I learn the Arabic Language? What is the way?

We want our students to graduate with a well grounded grasp of the Arabic Language. We aim to help them develop in the following areas which we believe are key and vital for a solid primary development.

1. Reading.
2. Writing.
3. Speaking.
4. Listening.

There are many aspects that come under these four main categories which we have chosen to focus on. I have decided to choose these four because of my past struggles that I had as a student of the Arabic Language and the problems that I faced when teaching this amazing language.

We want to, in our programme of books, develop the student's understanding in the four above areas *In Sha Allah*. A teacher can only show the student the way but he cannot force the student to learn. In the end of the day with the help of **Allāh** the student has to put in effort outside of his academic lessons.

The main purpose of a Muslim's life is worship. The reward is Paradise. We hope **Allāh** allows all of our works to be sincere for Him only and that he grants us a good ending.

We ask **Allāh** that he allows all of our works to benefit the local and international communities who are in great need of becoming reconnected to this amazing language which will help them become connected with the Words of **Allāh**.

*Written by the Servant of **Allāh**:*
K. A.
(Author & Teacher of Arabic & Islamic Sciences)

The Path of Knowledge or The Path of Ignorance?

A small brief treatise discussing a blessing from the blessings of **Allāh**: *(Knowledge).*

Independent P 1441 hijri

K. A.

1441 hijri

A draft copy for the Students of the Arabic Language. If you find any scientific or printing or any type of mistake please inform the one who gave you this book or your local centre.

سلسلة شروع ومؤلفات: (الموضوعات العامة)

Series of Publications 1441 h (Private Education)

A message for our Private Education students: If you happen to find any printing or scientific errors within this book please contact your centre or the author

The Path of Knowledge or The Path of Ignorance?

*A small brief treatise discussing a blessing from the blessings of **Allāh**: (Knowledge).*

*Ibn Al-Mubarak (may **Allāh** have mercy on him) said:*

"I do not know of anything after Prophethood more virtuous than spreading knowledge".

May Allah make us sincere until we meet Him, may He forgive our errors, may He allow our works to be accepted, may Allah forgive and wipe out our sins, may He rectify our private & public affairs, may He rectify our relationship with Him, may He protect us always, may He grant us a good ending & may He make our graves a garden from the gardens of Paradise.

كتب أُخرى قريبا إن شاء الله:

Other books available or soon to be available (if Allah wills):

- الشريعة والأركان شرح الفقه الأكبر لأبي حنيفة النعمان.

- The Legislation And Explanation of The Greatest Shari`ah (Arabic).

- الريان شرح لأحكام الصيام بأدلة القرآن وسنة رسول الرحمن ﷺ.

- Ar-Rayyān - Explanation of Rulings of the Fast (Arabic).

- الشرح المختصر العلمي (شرح) مختصر القدوري كتاب الصوم.

- A Summarised Explanation of Mukhtasar al-Quduri Vol 1 (Arabic).

- أبابيل شرح مختصر صحيح محمد بن إسماعيل (المجلد الأول).

- Abābīl: Vol 1 - Explanation of Sahih al-Bukhari (Arabic).

- الغربية عقيدة أهل السنة والجماعة.

- Al-Gharbiyyah (Arabic).

- فهم القواعد (نسخ كثيرة).

- Fahm Al-Qawaid.

The Path of Knowledge or The Path of Ignorance?
*A small brief treatise discussing a blessing from the blessings of **Allāh**: (Knowledge).*

- كتابة اللغة العربية (الحروف).

  - The Learning How to Write Arabic Book.

- شرح العقيدة الطحاوية المجلد ١ باللغة الإنجليزية.

  - Explanation of At-Tahawiyyah Volume 1 (English).

- برنامج اللغة العربية (الكلمات) ١.

  - `alamiyyah Arabic Course Book 1 (Arabic).

- برنامج اللغة العربية (الكلمات) ٢.

  - `alamiyyah Arabic Course Book 2 (Arabic).

- كتاب للحفظ.

  - Hifz Log Book.

- دعوة الأنبياء باللغة الإنجليزية.

  - The Prophet's Divine Message (English).

- رسائل لطلاب الجامعة باللغة الإنجليزية.

  - 6 Academic Essays (English).

The Path of Knowledge or The Path of Ignorance?

*A small brief treatise discussing a blessing from the blessings of **Allāh**: (Knowledge).*

- النعمة شرح عقيدة الأمة.

- The Blessing (Arabic).

- شجرة النحو ١.

- The Tree of Arabic Grammar 1 (Arabic).

- في سبيل العلم أو في سبيل الجهل؟

- The Path of Knowledge or The Path of Ignorance? (English).

- وغيرها قريبا إن شاء الله.

- Other books (if **Allāh** wills).

─────────(✷✷✷)─────────

في سبيل العلم

أو

في سبيل الجهل؟

(باللغة الإنجليزية)

البرنامج العالمي الأكاديمي - دراسة خاصة

تأليف الفقير إلى الله:

خادم الدين بن يونس بن عبد القادر

السريع

غفر الله له ولوالديه وللمسلمين

مشروع دار عقيدة الإسلام للنشر والتوزيع

The Path of Knowledge or The Path of Ignorance?

*A small brief treatise discussing a blessing from the blessings of **Allāh**: (Knowledge).*

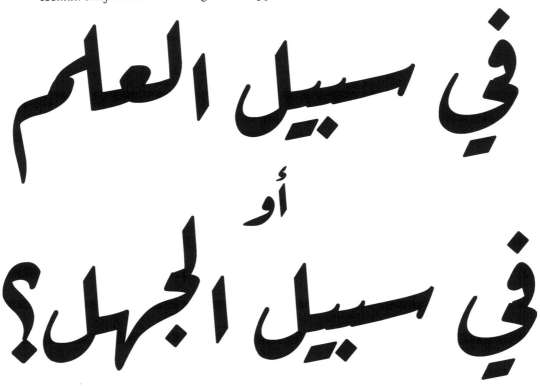

في سبيل العلم

أو

في سبيل الجهل؟

(باللغة الإنجليزية)

البرنامج العالمي الأكاديمي - دراسة خاصة

تأليف الفقير إلى الله:

خادم الدين بن يونس بن عبد القادر

السريع

غفر الله له ولوالديه وللمسلمين

مشروع دار عقيدة الإسلام للنشر والتوزيع

The Path of Knowledge or The Path of Ignorance?
A small brief treatise discussing a blessing from the blessings of **Allāh**: *(Knowledge).*

The Contents Page

The Path of Knowledge or The Path of Ignorance?
A small brief treatise discussing a blessing from the blessings of **Allāh**: *(Knowledge).*
The Path of Knowledge or The Path of Ignorance?
A small brief treatise discussing a blessing from the blessings of **Allāh**: *(Knowledge).*
The Path of Knowledge or The Path of Ignorance?
A small brief treatise discussing a blessing from the blessings of **Allāh**: *(Knowledge).*

The Path of Knowledge or The Path of Ignorance?
A small brief treatise discussing a blessing from the blessings of **Allāh**: *(Knowledge).*

The Path of Knowledge or The Path of Ignorance?

A small brief treatise discussing a blessing from the blessings of **Allāh**: *(Knowledge).*

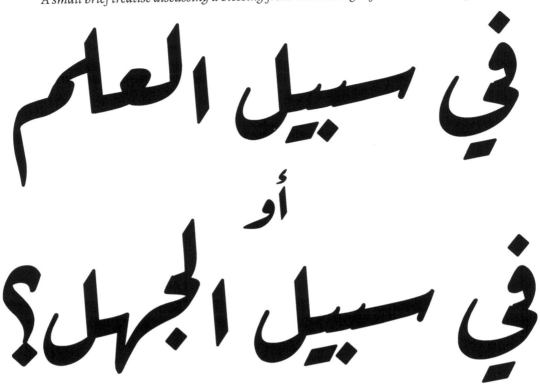

في سبيل العلم

أو

في سبيل الجهل؟

(باللغة الإنجليزية)

البرنامج العالمي الأكاديمي - دراسة خاصة

تأليف الفقير إلى الله:

خادم الدين بن يونس بن عبد القادر

السريع

غفر الله له ولوالديه وللمسلمين

مشروع دار عقيدة الإسلام للنشر والتوزيع

A Few Words

بسم الله الرحمن الرحيم

In the Name of Allāh the Most Gracious the Most Merciful

الحمد لله الحي القيوم الذي علم بالقلم و علم الإنسان ما لم يعلم وصلى الله على المصطفى محمد بن عبد الله صلى الله عليه و على آله و صحبه وسلم أما بعد:

Indeed all praise belongs (and is due to) to **Allāh** alone, we seek His help and His forgiveness. We seek refuge with **Allāh** from the evil of our own souls. Whomsoever **Allāh** guides none can lead astray and whomsoever **Allāh** leaves astray no one can guide. I bear witness that there is no deity worthy of worship except **Allāh** alone and I bear witness that Muḥammad is His slave and His Messenger.

`Abdullah bin Mas`ūd (may Allāh have mercy on him) said: "Knowledge is not having a large amount of Knowledge but Knowledge is having fear (of Allāh)". May Allāh grant us fear of Him and may He grant us a good ending. May Allāh make our graves a garden from the Gardens of Paradise.

أسأل الله الكريم رب العرش العظيم أن ينفع العالم والمسلمين كلهم بهذا العمل الصغير وأن يكتب لنا حسن الخاتمة وأن يكتب لهذا الكتاب القبول في الأرض وأن يغفر لنا ولإخواننا وأبنائنا وزوجاتنا ووالدينا وأن يدخلنا الجنة بغير عذاب ولا حساب.

The Path of Knowledge or The Path of Ignorance?

A small brief treatise discussing a blessing from the blessings of **Allāh**: *(Knowledge).*

وصلى الله على نبينا محمد وعلى آله وأصحابه أجمعين.

تأليف الفقير إلى الله:

خادم الدين بن يونس بن عبد القادر

السريع

غفر الله له ولوالديه وللمسلمين

© *1441 Hijri*

We are non-partisan. We do not support extremism.
We spread moderation through our academic lessons & courses.
There is no place or room for terrorism in our community work & projects.
Education is the cure for ignorance.

The Path of Knowledge or The Path of Ignorance?

*A small brief treatise discussing a blessing from the blessings of **Allāh**: (Knowledge).*

بسم الله الرحمن الرحيم

الحمد لله رب العالمين والصلاة والسلام على أشرف الأنبياء والمرسلين نبينا محمد وعلى آله وأصحابه أجمعين:

A Blessing

- Knowledge is a blessing from the blessings of **Allāh**.

- There is no doubt that if we were to count the blessings of **Allāh** we will not be able to count them.

- There is no doubt that the gift of Monotheism (*tawḥīd*) is the greatest blessing a person has been granted.

- Having knowledge is a blessing and if we want to understand the greatest blessing, build the greatest blessing and pass it on then we need knowledge.

- Islamic Knowledge is vital for your current and next life.

- Worldly knowledge is vital for this life however if used properly and sincerely it can help you for the next life.

○ Learning medicine and becoming a doctor is financially rewarding. If it is done with the correct intention linking it to aiding people for the pleasure of **Allāh** it can then become rewarding for the next life.

The Path of Knowledge or The Path of Ignorance?

*A small brief treatise discussing a blessing from the blessings of **Allāh**: (Knowledge).*

﴿وَإِن تَعُدُّوا نِعْمَةَ اللَّهِ لَا تُحْصُوهَا إِنَّ اللَّهَ لَغَفُورٌ رَّحِيمٌ﴾

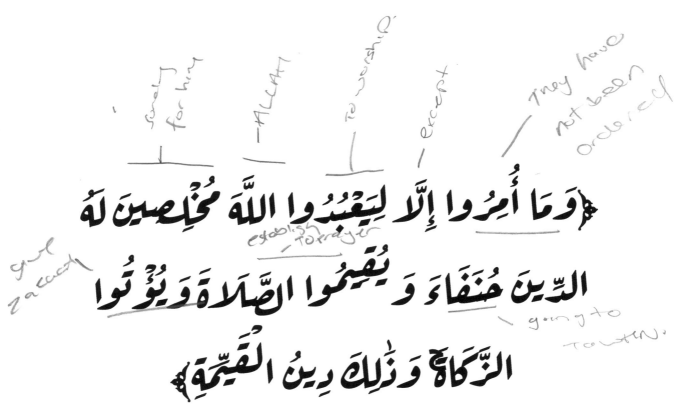

﴿وَمَا أُمِرُوا إِلَّا لِيَعْبُدُوا اللَّهَ مُخْلِصِينَ لَهُ الدِّينَ حُنَفَاءَ وَيُقِيمُوا الصَّلَاةَ وَيُؤْتُوا الزَّكَاةَ وَذَٰلِكَ دِينُ الْقَيِّمَةِ﴾

*EIMAAN Statements
- QOLON (SPEECH)
- AMALON (ACTION)
- ITIKAT. (implement belief).*

Sincerity

- We must try and purify our intentions for the sake of **Allāh** when doing ~~going~~ good deeds.

- This purification of intention is also for seeking knowledge.

- Seeking knowledge is truly a great thing for the one who has purified his intention.

- Scholars like Sufyan ath-Thawri (may **Allāh** have mercy on him) would mention the difficulty of treating and the hardship of dealing with the intention & how severe that was.

- Having faith is belief, statements and deeds.

- Your deeds will not be accepted without sincerity.

- Islam is not a business of this world and it is not something to be used to gain glitter, wealth, fame and positions.

- The one who does seek it for that will truly be humiliated because we have to seek it & spread it for the sake of **Allāh**.

- May **Allāh** make us from those who are sincere.

إِنَّمَا الأَعْمَالُ بِالنِّيَّاتِ وَإِنَّمَا لِكُلِّ امْرِئٍ مَا نَوَى

فَمَنْ كَانَتْ هِجْرَتُهُ إِلَى دُنْيَا يُصِيبُهَا أَوْ إِلَى

امْرَأَةٍ يَنْكِحُهَا فَهِجْرَتُهُ إِلَى مَا هَاجَرَ إِلَيْهِ

Young People & Knowledge

- There is no doubt in my mind that when young Muslims in the West and in the East begin learning Islamic Knowledge it will be the beginning that will help them face the current and upcoming challenges.

- Knowledge is one of the aspects that will help them deal with the different burdens and difficulties in their lives.

- This is true if Islamic Knowledge is learnt properly and then applied correctly.

- Many young people are facing serious issues in regards to their faith.

- Some youth due to ignorance abandon their faith.

- Some do so due to the challenges they face at secondary school or college or university.

- Simple doubts of the youth can be removed if they simply just ask those who know and those who they trust.

- If the youth knew that all their answers were in Islam it would bring them closer to **Allāh**.

- Sadly due to ignorance the youth have connected Islam with backwardness and superstitions.

The Path of Knowledge or The Path of Ignorance?

*A small brief treatise discussing a blessing from the blessings of **Allāh**: (Knowledge).*

- Every question that an Atheist or a Christian or a Muslim has then know dear reader that the answers have been adequately recorded and discussed.

- Islam has all the answers & solutions to your problems.

﴿وَمَا أَرْسَلْنَا قَبْلَكَ إِلَّا رِجَالًا نُّوحِي إِلَيْهِمْ فَاسْأَلُوا أَهْلَ الذِّكْرِ إِن كُنتُمْ لَا تَعْلَمُونَ﴾

﴿وَقَالُوا لَوْ كُنَّا نَسْمَعُ أَوْ نَعْقِلُ مَا كُنَّا فِي أَصْحَابِ السَّعِيرِ﴾

Knowledge From Leaving The Womb To Entering The Tomb

○ Every Muslim who is reading this must try & continue learning Islamic Knowledge until they die.

○ Certainly the connection, staying linked to knowledge & it's people will be a cause from the causes that will save you from destruction (if **Allāh** wills).

○ This Islamic Knowledge is part of your success and that includes implementation. Quality is important.

○ Your success in this life and the next is in following the Path of the Prophet ﷺ.

○ The four principles of success for this life and the next are:

1. **Knowledge.**   Surah Asr

2. **Action.**

3. *da`wah* **(inviting others to Islam).**

4. **Patience.**

○ May Allah make us from the people of success in this world and the next.

○ As Muslims we should be attached to knowledge from the first moments we are taught until our very last moments of this life (until our soul leaves this body).

The Path of Knowledge or The Path of Ignorance?
A small brief treatise discussing a blessing from the blessings of **Allāh**: *(Knowledge).*

o There was a man who died and left this world while reciting the Book of **Allāh**. What an amazing ending but not everyone is granted such a great ending.

o A child deserves a life of *tarbiyyah* and the child does not deserve to be thrown in front of the television or computer screen unattended.

o It is the child's right upon us that we give that child adequate solid foundational knowledge.

o Parents are not responsible for the outcome of their children if they did their job properly.

o The parent is responsible for planting, nurturing and aiding that son or daughter.

o As long as that child is under the parent's legal Islamic guardianship there is a huge amount of responsibility upon the shoulders of the parent.

o If you value the life of an individual then give that individual adequate education. Start with your family.

The Path of Knowledge or The Path of Ignorance?

*A small brief treatise discussing a blessing from the blessings of **Allāh**: (Knowledge).*

كُلُّكُمْ رَاعٍ وَكُلُّكُمْ مَسْؤُولٌ عَنْ رَعِيَّتِهِ

Connecting The Youth With The Qur`ān

- Children should be given the gift of the *Qur`an* very early on in their lives.

- Rewards such as sweets and toys should be given in order to make the *Qur`an* beloved to the child.

- Children should be accustomed to the *Qur`an* as they are accustomed to rhymes in school. It should be done greater than that.

- If children see you read, learn and play with them then this will have a huge impact on them.

- This impact will last permanently (if **Allāh** wills).

- Learning while a person is young will carve a permanent or long lasting impact.

- I remember my father, may **Allāh** have mercy on him and forgive him, taking me to the *masjid* when I was a young child.

- He did not allow me to leave his company and misbehave in the back of the *masjid* with the other children.

- This has had a huge impact on me personally.

- My mother, may **Allāh** preserve her & forgive her, would give me money every Friday to put in the *masjid* collection box.

The Path of Knowledge or The Path of Ignorance?

A small brief treatise discussing a blessing from the blessings of **Allāh***: (Knowledge).*

- ○ When I grew up my mother paid a huge amount of money for my education & studies at university which led me to where I am today (by **Allāh's** permission).

- ○ These moments that I have recorded in my mind have lasted and will last until I die (if **Allāh** wills).

- ○ This shows the importance and the huge impact parents have on their children.

﴿وَنَزَّلْنَا عَلَيْكَ الْكِتَابَ تِبْيَانًا لِكُلِّ شَيْءٍ وَهُدًى وَرَحْمَةً وَبُشْرَى لِلْمُسْلِمِينَ﴾

The Value Of Islamic Knowledge

- In a time that we live in today people have lost the value of Islamic Knowledge.

- People flee to & run to what shines and glitters.

- You find this today in our societies. A young person today drowns hours online and can barely explain the meaning of the *shahadah*.

- لا إله إلا الله There is no god worthy of worship in Truth except **Allāh**.

- Through my years of teaching and educating I have come across children who have passed the age of 11 still trying to learn the Arabic alphabet. No doubt they will be rewarded for trying but why are we in this situation?

- The Prophet ﷺ has told us in an authentic narration that the best of you is the one who learns the *Qur`an* and teaches it.

- Everyone will one day know the value of authentic beneficial knowledge. We hope that we learn and act before it is too late.

- We ask **Allāh** that He grants us beneficial knowledge and that He grants us steadfastness.

The Path of Knowledge or The Path of Ignorance?
*A small brief treatise discussing a blessing from the blessings of **Allāh**: (Knowledge).*

﴿قُلْ هَلْ يَسْتَوِي الَّذِينَ يَعْلَمُونَ وَالَّذِينَ لَا يَعْلَمُونَ إِنَّمَا يَتَذَكَّرُ أُولُو الْأَلْبَابِ﴾

Knowledge Helps To Build Fear

- Sound Knowledge allows a person to build fear of **Allāh**.

- Indeed only those who (truly) fear **Allāh** from amongst His slaves are the scholars.

- Many times we forget or disregard the outcomes of our actions due to ignorance or forgetfulness or a lack of fear or other reasons which the dear reader may know or may not know about.

- The prohibited will always remain prohibited even if the entire world does it. May **Allāh** allow us to remain upon the principles of Islam without compromising.

- If we are connected to knowledge and allow it to pass the stage of just being information, allowing it to impact us by actions it will help to instill fear.

- The true scholars of the *millah of* Islām are those who truly fear **Allāh**.

- We have scholars of the people, the scholars of the leader and then we have the true scholars who are the scholars of the Religion like the four great Imams.

The Path of Knowledge or The Path of Ignorance?

*A small brief treatise discussing a blessing from the blessings of **Allāh**: (Knowledge).*

Extremism & Looseness

- There is no doubt that beneficial Knowledge in a time of extremism, trials, tribulations and looseness will help keep a person steadfast.

- It is recorded that Shu'bah (may **Allāh** have mercy on him) travelled for a complete month seeking a *ḥadīth* (narration) he heard from a route that he did not come across.

- Knowledge will help to protect you from extremism and looseness if you are sincere.

- Knowledge will also help you to protect yourself unlike wealth which is something that you have to protect.

- A life of actions based upon ignorance will lead to difficulties & calamities.

The Path of Knowledge or The Path of Ignorance?

A small brief treatise discussing a blessing from the blessings of **Allāh**: *(Knowledge).*

Knowledge And Coming Closer To Allah

○ Knowledge if sought and learnt sincerely will bring you closer to **Allāh**.

○ When you know what **Allāh** loves this will lead you to try and do it and thus you will become beloved to **Allāh**.

○ Knowledge teaches us that a slave can come closer to **Allāh** and the best way to come closer to **Allāh** is by doing the obligations.

The Path of Knowledge or The Path of Ignorance?
*A small brief treatise discussing a blessing from the blessings of **Allāh**: (Knowledge).*

مَا تَقَرَّبَ إِلَيَّ عَبْدِي بِشَيْءٍ أَحَبَّ إِلَيَّ مِمَّا افْتَرَضْتُهُ عَلَيهِ

The Sweetness & Struggles In The Path of Knowledge

- The path & life of knowledge is indeed a sweet path and a difficult path.

- Look how the Companions struggled and suffered for the sake of **Allāh**.

- Their sacrifice helped to aid and spread this Religion.

- Some of us were given this Religion and we were taught by our parents without any sacrifice.

- Look at the great efforts of Abu Hurairah (may **Allāh** be pleased with him) who narrated so many narrations.

- You may be poor or may have to spend upon this path but consider that a test and a reward from **Allāh**.

- **Allāh** knows what is good for you and what is not good for you.

- **Allāh** knows what is best for you so leave everything with **Allāh.**

The Path of Knowledge or The Path of Ignorance?

*A small brief treatise discussing a blessing from the blessings of **Allāh**: (Knowledge).*

Make some effort

- Some people learn Islamic Knowledge so they can be called an *'ālim* or *qāri`*.

- This kind of intention if kept and continued upon will be an intention that will lead to Hell.

- There is a hidden desire among humans who do good works. You will find this amongst Muslims and non-Muslims.

- What is this hidden desire that is within? It is that a person would like others to know about their good deeds. May **Allāh** save us from this attribute.

- Having followers & subscribers on facebook, twitter, youtube and other social networks is a trial for the one being followed.

- We ask **Allāh** to clean our hearts and yours hearts from the sickness of wanting fame through Religion.

- There is no doubt at all that the early pious generations were the furthest away from wanting fame.

- The sincere people of the past would wish their knowledge could spread without it being referenced to them.

- Truly it can be said as the Pious of the past would say, the one who loves fame has not feared **Allāh**.

- In reality if a Muslim knows what his spiritual status is, he does not really care if the people think he is religous or not.

- His only concern is **Allāh**.

- People today do not want to make an effort for knowledge.

- For a nice restaurant that serves nice food people will travel from a city to another but for knowledge they will not make the same effort.

- Distractions have also become many.

- Knowledge is really something that one goes to, which shows the great respect for what is taught.

- Knowledge does not come. That was definitely true in the past. Today with the advanced developments scholars travel from country to country to teach us.

- Knowledge has become accessible through books, online classes, audio and video.

- What excuse do we have?

Gatherings

○ The benefits of the gatherings of knowledge are numerous.

○ One will find in circles of knowledge brotherhood, a chance to humble oneself, tranquility, good influence, knowledge, manners and sweetness.

○ One must come to such gatherings of knowledge seeking **Allāh's** pleasure.

○ Whoever is sincere for **Allāh**, **Allāh** will open the doors of good for this individual.

○ One of the beneficial ways to revise when you are distracted is turn off the internet access.

○ You can go to a room in your house or a quiet part of the library or an office or somewhere where you can sit and revise.

○ You can sit with another serious pious student to learn with.

○ Sometimes this kind of seclusion can protect a person, it can give him time to read, write and learn.

○ We must try and learn Islamic Knowledge and apply it as much as possible before we become preoccupied.

○ Have high aims. Have lofty goals.

○ Make *jannat al-firdous* your target even if you have to tread it alone.

The Path of Knowledge or The Path of Ignorance?

*A small brief treatise discussing a blessing from the blessings of **Allāh**: (Knowledge).*

o Some Prophets had no followers and some had a few.

o Take the path of knowledge and sweetness and take advantage of your time before you have to pay bills, before you have to take care of your future family, before you have obligations and other responsibilities.

o Analyse your situation and then see how you can seek Knowledge in the available time and opportunities you have available.

o There is a lot of knowledge and opportunity in your country.

o So try to drink from the knowledge in your country.

o Lay down your goals and try and achieve them.

o O dear brothers and sisters never underestimate yourself. If you have **Allāh** with you can achieve anything.

o A Muslim and especially the student of knowledge must be an all rounded person to the best of his ability.

o He must understand the problems of the times he lives in. It is not enough for every Muslim just to have knowledge. Knowledge, implementation & steadfastness.

o As an ideal student and leader you need to have a profession. This will help the student of knowledge become independent.

o If you are independent financially and not stuck then you can overcome the statement "you cannot bite the hand that feeds you".

Loving praise

○ As a student you should not love to be praised for things you did not do.

○ There is no doubt that loving praise and recommendation is from the avenues which the devil uses to enter into.

○ So self amazement, stinginess and following a yearning lust are from the things that will destroy a person.

○ These are characteristics a student of knowledge should stay away from. May **Allāh** protect me and you because if **Allāh** does not protect us then there is no protection.

○ Today on social networks people like to pretend that they are living happy lives.

○ Many people who show others on facebook or twitter externally that they are happy are suffering from depression.

○ All of us have a deficiency in obeying **Allāh** so we should work on this deficiency and avoid pretending on social networks about having a life of an angel.

○ A person should never praise himself, he should not attach titles to his name that he does not deserve.

The Path of Knowledge or The Path of Ignorance?
*A small brief treatise discussing a blessing from the blessings of **Allāh**: (Knowledge).*

o Whoever rushes something before its due time will be punished through being prevented from that thing.

o If a person has knowledge and he does not implement this knowledge then it will be a proof against him on the Day of Judgement.

o The scholars mention that applying the knowledge will aid a person in carving that knowledge within one's memory.

o *zakāt* of wealth is 2.5% with the required fulfilled conditions. *zakat* of knowledge is that you act upon it and teach it.

o Knowledge, then action, then propagation and then patience.

o The devil wants to take me, you and every human to Hell.

o The devil does not care about nationality, your status, your colour, your language or anything else. He wants us to join him as human beings in Hell forever.

o Students of knowledge are a light and source of benefit wherever they go.

o This benefit is for every human.

Our Ignorance

- A person will go to Paradise according to a narration for quenching the thirst of an animal. What do you think about quenching the thirst of a human being? Small actions can take you very far.

- When we try to fool people to present an image that is contrary to the truth there will be an inner feeling of uneasiness.

- As humans the knowledge that we have is only a little.

- We discovered recently around 2018 CE that the firehawk (a bird) makes fires worse by picking up branches of fire and starting fires in other places. The Prophet ﷺ told us that there is no harm in killing such animals. These are dangerous animals.

- The point is that humans are always discovering new things which shows the level of our ignorance.

- You will meet some people, some *shaykhs*, some relatives, some colleagues and some friends that try to lower you and divert you from trying to reach your potential.

- Some people want you to stay low so they can be high.

- The solution is never underestimate yourself.

The Path of Knowledge or The Path of Ignorance?

*A small brief treatise discussing a blessing from the blessings of **Allāh**: (Knowledge).*

- If you are sincere you will be able to do wonders regardless of the weakness of your memory, understanding, your financial and physical situation. Success is with **Allāh** not with humans.

- Students of knowledge are from the best of people.

- The devil will try to harm students and the pious with more effort compared to his efforts with ordinary people.

- Constantly reading and studying is a solution to forgetting. Always be connected to **the Creator**, Islam, knowledge & study when you are able.

- It is known to all students of knowledge that leaving of sins is a reason that helps the memory.

- Your time is set. We have to try to take advantage of our time. This will help us in seeking knowledge, it will help us also in gaining success in both worlds.

- We have to beware of procrastination.

- If you have children start helping them memorise early from as young as possible. Play the *Qur`an* in their presence.

Time

- Time is more valuable than gold, just ask the billionaires what they say about time.

- One billionaire said "time is the only thing I cannot buy".

- If you look at some of the scholars when they sit between questions or between translations they would engage in *istighfār*.

- They would not waste any time, they would engage in the remembrance of **Allāh**. I have seen this with my own eyes on many occasions.

- Some of the scholars of the past you will not find them except that they were reading or revising or that they had a book in their hand.

- Everyday that goes past that is a part of us gone and it will never come back.

- Time will never ever return. It is impossible.

- The Pious Predecessors were very eager indeed in taking advantage and using their time wisely.

- If we measure the time we benefit from and the time we waste we will find a great difference in terms of measurement.

The Path of Knowledge or The Path of Ignorance?
A small brief treatise discussing a blessing from the blessings of **Allāh***: (Knowledge).*

- There is nothing wrong with mixing and socialising with brothers. There is nothing wrong with visits and trips. However we should try to ask **Allāh** to help us to utilise this valuable time.

- Some people spend hours with their friends daily. There must be a strong sense of brotherhood however one needs to remember regularly that we should try to be cautious of time

- The devil will deceive us by making us think that we have done a lot.

- The devil will say to you, you are better than others so relax.

- Then we will find that the time of relaxation was far beyond and became a great deal of waste.

- One has to understand that knowledge is not about narrating a lot but it is a light **Allāh** puts in the heart.

- Look at the devil, see how he had so much knowledge but it did not benefit him.

Value

○ When you test something that is permissible then you will know the value of something.

○ I am referring to the importance of the media.

○ There is a great deal of benefit in using audio and video live lessons to supplement other avenues of learning.

○ There is no doubt knowledge is a blessing. These audio lessons, sermons & lectures are also a blessing.

○ There are 2 young students in the United Kingdom who were able to memorise 2-3 Juz of Qur'an by **Allāh's** permission then by listening to Muhammad Siddīq al-Minshāwī (may **Allāh** have mercy on him).

○ This indicates us towards the value of audio lessons and benefitting from audio recordings.

○ When you get married and have children you will become extremely busy.

○ Use your free time even if it is with small actions of learning and worship.

○ Single life and married life are both stressful. It is about making most of what you have.

The Path of Knowledge or The Path of Ignorance?

A small brief treatise discussing a blessing from the blessings of **Allāh**: *(Knowledge).*

○ As a student seclusion is important. You need some time during the week and possibly daily to think and contemplate about the course of action.

○ The pious people of the past (and we are most certainly far away from their way) used to leave the taste and pleasure of sleep staying awake during the nights to seek Islamic Knowledge

○ Knowledge is a light which **Allāh** puts in the heart. It is not about reading & reciting however it is a light that **Allāh** places.

○ Fear of **Allāh** is also a fruit from the fruits of Islamic Knowledge.

Final words

○ If a slave combines sincerity and the causes of deeds then indeed the slave will be able to do what was almost impossible for him. If you have **Allāh**, He is sufficient.

○ If you are poor **Allāh** will make you self sufficient.

○ Dear brother, every Muslim needs sincerity, bodily effort, spending of time, struggling with his soul and even sometimes spending financially.

○ Imām adh-Dhahabī (may **Allāh** have mercy on him) mentions that in the gathering of Imām Ahmad (may **Allāh** have mercy on him) 5000 or more would gather.

○ 500 or so would write and the rest would learn good manners and praiseworthy silence.

○ There are many courses, lessons, circles and programmes today. We will regret it if we do not take full advantage of them.

○ Living amongst opportunities of knowledge is a great blessing and especially when the community you are living in is a practicing community.

○ The loss of scholars is indeed a great loss that money cannot replace.

○ This divine *risālat* is a message that gives life to the hearts.

55 Private Education - ***Project Madrasah Dār SEMA*** - *Make your notes using the blank space below:*

o The ones who have replaced the gatherings of knowledge for gatherings of corruption & gossip are like the ones who have exchanged that which is better for that which is lower.

o Some of the Pious Predecessors would say "If one day would pass me by and I did not increase in knowledge on that day then that day was not made blessed for me".

o It is better to be stingy with your time then being stingy with your money.

o **Money can never buy you more time.**

o We should go and return from circles of knowledge with sincerity.

o A Muslim will be rewarded if he struggles with his intention trying to be sincere for **Allāh**.

o Truly when a slave is eager and sincere (**Allāh** knows the truthfulness of his intention) **Allāh** will open up for him His blessings and make his affairs easy for him.

o We should not enumerate what we have attended from circles of knowledge because our ignorance is greater than our knowledge.

o If it was not for the help and aid of **Allāh** and His care much of our efforts would have not gained any fruits.

The Path of Knowledge or The Path of Ignorance?
*A small brief treatise discussing a blessing from the blessings of **Allāh**: (Knowledge).*

- Abu al-'Abbās Ahmad the scholar of Arabic Language said about Ibrahīm al-Harbī "I did not find Ibrahīm al-Harbī missing from a gathering (and lesson) of Grammar or Language for 50 years".

- When we were children we used to value every pound and penny we used to get. Similarly when we study we should value every lesson more than we value money.

- Imām ash-Shāfī (may **Allāh** have mercy on him) has mentioned that by not relying on anyone, travelling to the different countries, having patience like the patience of the donkey & the earliness of the earliness of the crow he was able to acquire this knowledge.

- Reading books and making brief notes are very beneficial.

- If a student continues to read books, continues to make notes and revise then he will attain a good level.

- **Only through trials will an individual learn and know.**

- In the gatherings of knowledge one should not talk, not make noise and not mess around with pens.

- A student should show signs of respect for the teacher and the gathering.

- **Life is short. Death is certain. The question is now how long you have left but what are you going to do with what you have left?**

Private Education

We also offer online lessons.

Join or Support Us.

How do I learn the Arabic Language? What is the way?

We want our students to graduate with a well grounded grasp of the Arabic Language. We aim to help them develop in the following areas which we believe are key and vital for a solid primary development.

5. Reading.
6. Writing.
7. Speaking.
8. Listening.

There are many aspects that come under these four main categories which we have chosen to focus on. I have decided to choose these four because of my past struggles that I had as a student of the Arabic Language and the problems that I faced when teaching this amazing language.

We want to, in our programme of books, develop the student's understanding in the four above areas *In Sha Allah*. A teacher can only show the student the way but he cannot force the student to learn. In the end of the day with the help of **Allāh** the student has to put in effort outside of his academic lessons.

The main purpose of a Muslim's life is worship. The reward is Paradise. We hope **Allāh** allows all of our works to be sincere for Him only and that he grants us a good ending. We ask **Allāh** that he allows all of our works to benefit the local and international communities who are in great need of becoming reconnected to this amazing language which will help them become connected with the Words of **Allāh**.

*Written by the Servant of **Allāh**:*
K. A.
(Author & Teacher of Arabic & Islamic Sciences)

The Path of Knowledge
or
The Path of Ignorance?

A small brief treatise discussing a blessing from the blessings of Allah: (Knowledge).

Project Madrasah Dār SEMA

`alamiyyah Academic Structured Islamic Education

If Allah wants good for you he will grant you understanding of the Religion.
Knowledge. Action. Invitation to the Message. Patience.

Knowledge

Modular Education For Higher Madrassah Academic Development & Thinking
The Academic `alamiyyah Seminary Programmes & Title Certification

`aqidah * fiqh * hadith * tafsir * Arabic * `usul * da`wah * other Sciences

Private Education

A teacher can teach you this book. This is a very basic level for your academic madrasah education part of the Higher Madrasah Education programme. We hope you will benefit from this small brief treatise.

The Path of Knowledge or The Path of Ignorance?

*A small brief treatise discussing a blessing from the blessings of **Allāh**: (Knowledge).*

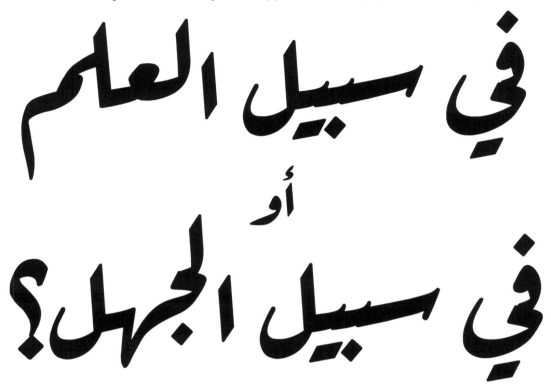

في سبيل العلم

أو

في سبيل الجهل؟

(باللغة الإنجليزية)

البرنامج العالمي الأكاديمي - دراسة خاصة

تأليف الفقير إلى الله:

خادم الدين بن يونس بن عبد القادر

السريع

غفر الله له ولوالديه وللمسلمين

اللهم اجعل هذا الكتاب نافعا مباركا واجعله سببا لهداية الغافلين والمسلمين والناس أجمعين

Printed in Poland
by Amazon Fulfillment
Poland Sp. z o.o., Wrocław